Come Sit Awhile

'In these pages, we see Taylor's remarkable gift of elevating the ordinary to something special, something poetic, even ...'
Irish Independent on *The Women*

'It's like sitting and having a big warm blanket wrapped around you ...'
Cork Today with Patricia Messinger on *Tea for One*

For more books by Alice Taylor, see obrien.ie

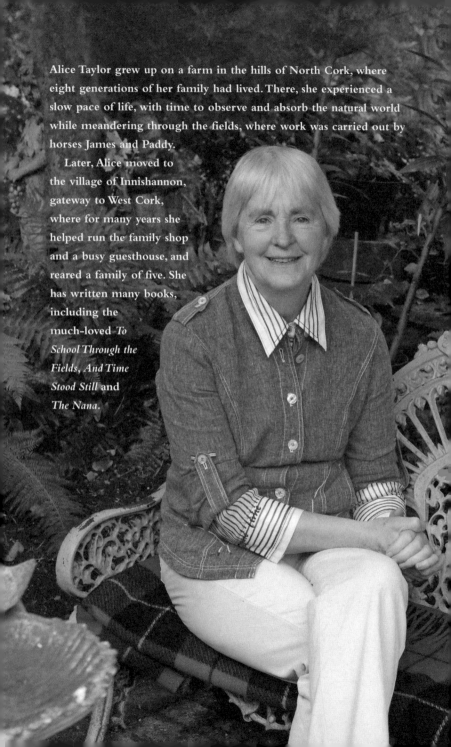

Alice Taylor grew up on a farm in the hills of North Cork, where eight generations of her family had lived. There, she experienced a slow pace of life, with time to observe and absorb the natural world while meandering through the fields, where work was carried out by horses James and Paddy.

Later, Alice moved to the village of Innishannon, gateway to West Cork, where for many years she helped run the family shop and a busy guesthouse, and reared a family of five. She has written many books, including the much-loved *To School Through the Fields*, *And Time Stood Still* and *The Nana*.

Come Sit Awhile

Alice Taylor

Photographs by Emma Byrne

BRANDON

First published 2023 by Brandon, an imprint of The O'Brien Press Ltd.
12 Terenure Road East, Rathgar, Dublin 6, D06 HD27, Ireland.
Tel: +353 1 4923333 Fax: +353 1 4922777
Email: books@obrien.ie. Website: obrien.ie
The O'Brien Press is a member of Publishing Ireland.

ISBN 978-1-78849-453-3

Printed bound by
Drukarnia Skleniarz, Poland.

The paper used in this book is produced
using pulp from managed forests.

Published in:

Dedication

For Reese
who loved all things bright and beautiful

Contents

Let's Light a Candle

There are times in life when we all need the presence of another human being. Maybe to sit together in silent companionship, to discuss something that is bothering us, to chat quietly about a shared interest or to enjoy an old joke. Covid robbed us of these interactions, resulting in a certain social withdrawal that is very slowly righting itself. There is a lot of wisdom in the Ralph Waldo Emerson quote: 'Go often to the house of thy friend, for weeds choke up the unused path.' How energising it is when an old friend calls by and you sit together enjoying a meeting of minds which leaves you feeling lighter. Even a phone chat can help move you forward.

But there are other days when friends are not available and we find it difficult to apply ourselves to what we need to do – and at such times the writings of somebody who experienced a similar situation to ourselves may echo in our mind and help us see a little kink of light that leads us on. Having a small treasury of such moments is a comfort that I cultivate. When we feel abandoned and not able to concentrate, the words of an old familiar poem, hymn or prayer can trickle into our minds and switch us back into gear. I keep a journal and also write little poems to capture fleeting moments.

> How nice to sit and think awhile
> Of little things to make you smile,
> Happy things you did in fun
> Long ago when you were young. …

This book is about taking time out, time to think, time to lift ourselves out of our everyday busy-ness. Along these pages we will recall stories, experiences and thoughts, and sometimes engage with wiser minds than mine to share words that have comforted many down through the years and that I find particularly helpful. Our ancestors have left with us the wisdom of their time when life was lived close to nature and incorporated a respect for the earth and for a greater power.

> ... To think of people who were kind
> And left a ray of light behind,
> People who were nice to know
> When you were young long time ago.
>
> So come and sit with me awhile
> And think of things to make us smile.

Nature too can influence our sense of well-being. We have all known foggy, dull days when a low sky wraps a grey shroud around our shoulders and we trudge on, heavy-footed and glum-faced. And then comes a bright, sunny morning and unconsciously our step lightens, we move forward with a new sense of enthusiasm, a smile streams across our face – and suddenly it is good to be alive. We are hugely influenced by light.

Heat and light – what wonderful gifts that lift the spirit. It is so good to stop and soak them up. These moments are precious. Our ancestors knew this and

had the expertise, wisdom and foresight to create the wonder of light at Newgrange, and when St Patrick lit his symbolic fire on the hill of Tara he sent shock-waves across the pagan plains of Ireland. Cathedral creators, with their awareness of the human need for morning light, faced the windows above the sanctuaries eastwards so that the rising sun could pour in and light up the minds of praying people. The symbolism of candlelight, too, beams forth from all religious traditions. At Easter the Paschal candle is lit, and at Christmas the old Irish tradition of the welcoming candle is part of who we are. When Mary Robinson was president she placed a lighting candle in a window of Áras an Uachtaráin, shining forth a welcome to our diaspora. And when hardship and hunger forced entire families to emigrate from the depths of rural Ireland the last member to leave the old home took a burning sod to a neighbouring house, carrying with it the hope that one day someone would return to rekindle a flame in that now-abandoned hearth. The symbolism of that firelight kept alive a hope that eased the pain of the forced departure.

Nowadays, in our local church here in Innishannon,

a small candelabra constantly glows with little lighted candles. People slip in quietly to say a quick prayer and light a candle, and sometimes they pick up one of the little cards from a nearby shelf to let a friend in trouble know that a candle has been lit for them and that they are not forgotten. The comfort of this connectedness can help another keep going through tough times.

The day was long and dreary
And the burden I was carrying
Seemed heavier than I could bear.
But then suddenly it lifted,
And I did not know that
Someone had knelt in prayer!

Sometimes the words of a long-gone poet or pilgrim can raise us above the challenges of demanding days. In *Come Sit Awhile* we will share words that invoke the blessings of human, natural and divine light.

Morning Has Broken

For me these words from Eleanor Farjeon turn morning-time into a celebration, and light up a scene full of vibrant energy and fond memories. What a wonderful salutation they are to energise us into another day. Sunbeams sparkle along the dew-laden grass, awakening the blackbird to a bright new beginning. Alerted by the new light, he breaks into song. The world is waking up, encapsulating the energy and grace of sunrise.

Morning has broken,
Like the first morning,
Blackbird has spoken
Like the first bird;
Praise for the singing,

Praise for the morning,
Praise for them springing
Fresh from the Word.

With these words you sense the whole world waking up with exuberant energy and enthusiasm. I experience this as an energising alleluia to dance us into fresh beginnings. The song/poem lights up the mind.

Sweet the rain's new fall
Sunlit from heaven,
Like the first dewfall
On the first grass;
Praise for the sweetness
Of the wet garden,
Sprung in completeness
When his feet pass.

When I go out into the early-morning garden these lines dance around me. You get the sense that while you slept mystery had walked along the garden paths and the mystery of nature's bounty is about to unfold all through the day too.

Mine is the sunlight
Mine is the morning,
Born of the one light
Eden saw play;
Praise with elation,
Praise every morning,
God's recreation
Of the new day.

These energising and beautiful words are full of joy, and in them earth reflects heaven. They were much loved by my sister Ellen, which is why I often think of them. When sung in full choir the song salutes the wonder of nature, heaven and earth. Ellen loved it all her life and we sang it at her funeral service in Toronto where she died, and again later at the end of her final journey in Innishannon where she came back to rest in the place she so loved. On her headstone are inscribed the words 'Morning Has Broken'.

When I stand there now, I silently sing the words of this uplifting song. It is so lovely to ponder these thoughts in the early morning. What an enrichment to our world are people who leave behind such awareness. Thank you, Ellen!

Peace Prayer of St Francis

I always had a special *grá* for St Francis and he often makes himself present in quiet moments. Maybe this affection was planted in my childhood by a Franciscan cousin, Brother Matthew, who visited our farm with the folds of his brown habit hiding sweets, medals and holy pictures. The pictures of St Francis surrounded by animals and with birds resting on his hands echoed our own world on the remote mountainside farm, where we lived close to nature. That was a time when the Franciscans went begging from door to door in order to survive. Strangely enough, begging did not phase my cousin as in the process he got to know some wonderful people – and it also afforded him the opportunity to spread the peace message of St Francis in which he fervently believed:

Lord, make me an instrument of your peace:
where there is hatred,
let me sow love;
where there is injury, pardon;
where there is doubt, faith;
where there is despair, hope;
where there is darkness, light;
where there is sadness, joy.

When I got married Br Matthew gave me this prayer, beautifully framed to grace my new home. Occasionally over the years, I picked it up and read it, endeavouring to absorb some of its wisdom. Then some years ago I heard Sinéad O'Connor sing a beautiful rendering of it on 'The Late Late Show', and this took it to another level. I felt that St Francis had moved with the times and was now endeavouring to spread his peace in more up-to-date ways.

Some years ago I visited Assisi and brought home under my arm a statue of St Francis, which, during the summer, enjoys the garden and at Christmas guards the crib. It was Francis who instigated the practice of

erecting the crib at Christmas, a tradition I really love, so it is fitting that he should rotate between his two favourite venues.

When I am in dire straits, or anyone of the family or a friend has hit a rock, I write to the Poor Clare Sisters for support. The Poor Clares, where I have a cousin, Sr Anthony Mary, are a sister order of the Franciscans, founded at the same time in Assisi, so I feel that they are singing from the same hymn sheet as the Franciscans. And the Poor Clares invariably come good on my call for help. I probably inherited this habit from my mother, who, when things were tough, always wrote to the Poor Clares whom she got to know when our four-year-old little Connie died in the Bons Secours hospital in Cork, and she got great solace from the Poor Clares whose convent is next door to the hospital. They gave her a relic of St Thérèse of Lisieux, who was known as the 'Little Flower', and who promised that when she died she would pour down from Heaven a shower of beautifully scented pink roses. Over my childhood bed hung a picture of the Little Flower with a large bunch of pink roses, so I grew up beneath her flower shower. Back then there were no punk rockers or soccer stars to grace our bedroom walls!

Slow Me Down

Do you ever get so caught up in such a state of fast-forward confusion that you are not quite sure whether you are coming or going? Mentally flying around in such non-stop circles that you crash into yourself coming back? I certainly do, and the writer of this ancient prayer had definitely been there. But realisation had obviously dawned that this was a crazy way to live and that the time had come to slow down.

> Slow me down, Lord.
> Ease my pounding heart
> Quieten my racing mind.
> Steady my hurried steps…

As soon as I begin to read these words I feel my mind begin to slow down and as the prayer continues on its easing journey it paints a picture of the calming hills clearing away the daily confusion and recommending the magical restorative power of sleep – 'Sleep that knits up the ravell'd sleeve of care,' as Shakespeare put it.

This poem goes on its slowing-down journey with such calming recommendations that I always feel myself absorbed into its wisdom.

Teach me the art of taking time off,
Of slowing down to look at a flower.
To chat with a friend.
To read a few lines from a good book.

As I visit all these tranquil scenes I begin to wonder why on earth I had allowed myself to get so carried away on a self-destructive speed bubble. And, finally, the writer walks us under the branches of a giant oak and looking up at its great branches we realise that this tree took a very long time to grow – slowly – and that its solidity and strength were developed gradually. There is no quick route for an oak tree.

And the final words lead us into a calm, tranquil

Slow me down, Lord.
Teach me to be gentle
And humble of heart
That I might find rest
For my soul.

I keep a copy of this ancient piece of wisdom in my desk drawer to be pulled out when confusion reigns. And when I have completely lost the run of myself I post a copy of it on my kitchen door so that it hits me in the face and puts a stop to my gallop.

Waiting for Our Souls to Catch Up

I n recent years meditation has made a bit of a comeback. It encourages us to take time to slow down, resulting in a calmer approach to life, and I embrace its wisdom. Long ago, contemplation was more naturally incorporated into our slower way of life, but now its practice is a long haul and a high climb. Applying our bottoms to a chair to meditate for thirty minutes, or even for a few minutes, morning and evening, is a challenge beyond most of us. But I find that sitting still in a quiet place and repeating a monotonous mantra can really help slow down the restless mind. Sometimes, as soon as you begin to do this, a hundred things you *should* be doing stream into your consciousness. But it can help to begin with a centring prayer. Any choice that works for you is fine, but this is the one that I was taught at a meditation talk – and it works for me. Sometimes!

The following words are a translation of the 'Our Father' from the Aramaic. Here's how I journey through them in my efforts to find a meditative space.

Birther, father-mother of the cosmos
You create all that moves in light.

These words span the entire concept of creation and settle us down to accept being a little fragment of that immensity.

I find that the following words ease the grip of my racing mind thus helping create a space where a sense of soothing calmness erodes my desire for busy-ness.

Help us let go
Clear the space inside of busy forgetfulness.

Then we ease on to unity of creation where we become part of a greater whole:

Create your reign of unity now

Through our fiery hearts and willing hands

Then we deal with the basic needs of survival with which we constantly engross ourselves:

Grant what we need each day
In bread and insight
Subsistence for the call of growing life.

And finally we are encouraged to let go of the pointless exercises of the blame and regret game that blights most of our lives. The words encourage us instead to look below the surface of the trivialities that tangle up our lives and hold us back from deep peace of mind.

Loose the cords of mistakes binding us
As we release the strands we hold of others' guilt.
Don't let surface things delude us
But free us from what holds us back
From our true purpose.

The aim of this prayer is to clear the mind of all dross, which is easier said than done. It is best to take it in stages and I find that dividing up the words helps break down the process into those stages. This is most helpful in trying to find a meditative space. And after these centring words everyone can use their own mantra to slowly calm the mind even further.

But despite my best efforts to slow the mind down, there is often a busy little man with a hammer in there reminding me of everything I am trying to put to one side for now. He is determined to keep hammering away. Some days he may decide to go away and give me a break, but just when I begin to think I might have it mastered, he cracks back into action again.

In some ways meditation is a little like brushing your teeth – it has to become a habit. Constancy! It's all about the doing. Not reading about it, not listening to talks about it, just simply doing it. Simple, but not easy!

I love the following story about the value of slowing down. An entrepreneur ran himself into the ground and suffered from total burn-out, so he went off to a remote island where life moved at a different pace. The natives there enjoyed life at a slow pace, and very gradually the entrepreneur found himself adjusting to

their way of life and recovering his joy in living. Then one day he came upon a very rare and valuable substance which he knew would make him a fortune if he could get it back to the mainland. So he hired some of the natives to carry it on their backs to the port. Unaware of its value and maybe not really concerned about it they went along happily with his plan, working long hours but never losing their obvious joy in life. He was delighted with them and knew that if they kept moving at this pace he would reach the port in time to catch the last ship, which was vital for his get-rich-quick plan. But on the last morning he woke up to find all his helpers fast asleep, and he was unable to wake them up. But finally one man did wake up. In answer to the entrepreneur's demand to know what was happening, he said: 'For many days we travel. We travel too much and too fast. Now we need to rest and wait for our souls to catch up.'

Meditation is all about waiting for our souls to catch up!

A Ploughed Field

I was once stopped up by a ploughed field! It lifted me out of the everyday. A brown ploughed field darned along a hillside is like a miraculous medal on the bosom of Mother Earth. Here a blessed unity of nature, with the human and divine combine to produce the very bread of life. We have evolved from the ploughman and his horse to the modern man on his enormous John Deere, but both of them plough the same earth in preparation for planting. The ploughing and the planting are the first twosome in this wondrous trinity and then the third element, the divine miracle of growth, comes into play. This is why a farmer and a gardener are well aware of powers greater than themselves at work. We in Ireland with our remembrance of the Famine, know only too well the resulting trauma when these forces fail to come good. A ploughed field is a smile of trust on the face of the earth and a prayer of hope in the future.

Oh brown ploughed field,
What an ancient skill
Is in your turned sod,
A skill inherited
By generations of earthy men.

As you drive along a country road and see a ploughed field on a distant hill you are naturally connected to the life-giving importance of farming life. This skill that has been passed down through the ages is as vital today as it was when our ancestors dug the earth with a spade. A ploughed field peeping from between trees is a brown-cloaked mystery where the furrows, like the lines on the page of a copybook, hold a story yet to be written.

Beneath the sheltering trees
You cover the hillside
In a cloak of brown velvet.
What a softness is yours;
You are an open book
Yet to be written;

The virginity of the upturned sod
Waiting to be fertilised
By the hands of man
And nurtured by the warmth of nature.

The above poem was written in the most unlikely of circumstances. I was at an under-age football match with one of my clutch on the team and at the time I was one of those crazy mothers on the side-line bawling at the opposition and screaming at the referee to do a better job. It was springtime and suddenly on the hill opposite a ploughed field caught my eye – and the playing pitch disappeared to be replaced by the bigger mystery of the ploughed field. I came home with a ploughed field in my head.

Trees

Is there anything more awe-inspiring than a giant tree standing majestically in its own space? A space where it has the scope to display its stately trunk and to stretch out its giant branches. It is, indeed, a thing of beauty and a joy forever, and a salutation to the wonder of nature and the person who planted it. A tree may begin life as a little weak sapling but over the years it gathers momentum until it eventually bursts forth in a huge statement.

Inside the entrance gate to our church is a large copper beech planted in 1974 as a slender sapling by the then curate Fr Seamus Murphy. It is now an impressive presence enriching and enhancing its surroundings. Its majestic, stately stature demands attention and often causes me to stop and look at it in silent awe and admiration. When I take the time to stand back and look up at this tree the words of

Joyce Kilmer float into my mind:

> I think that I shall never see
> A poem lovely as a tree.

This is where poetry actually comes into its own because a poem can capture images and experiences in a very special and memorable way. As the words of this poem float into my mind, the poet too, though long gone, comes alive again in this homage to the tree. I am sharing the same mind-space with the writer. This is the magic of poetry. And in this poem the poet continues in his choice of words to bring to life the picture of a mother and child and then an image of a tree stretching out its broad branches in homage to creation.

> A tree whose hungry mouth is prest
> Against the earth's sweet flowing breast;

> A tree that looks at God all day
> And lifts her leafy arms to pray;

And then, though you may be standing by the tree in summer, the poet carries you through the wonder of all the seasons:

> A tree that may in Summer wear
> A nest of robins in her hair;

> Upon whose bosom snow has lain;
> Who intimately lives with rain.

And, finally, the humility of the poet makes you aware of our human limitations and the awesome power of the divine in creation.

> Poems are made by fools like me
> But only God can make a tree.

When we leave this earth what greater blessing can we leave on it than a tree? Thank you, Fr Seamus, for planting the wonderful copper beech.

I wonder might it be a good practice if instead of headstones we commemorated people with trees? Though the one thing in favour of headstones is that

they are a historical record whereas a tree is a silent commemoration. But maybe we could do both! How wonderful to be remembered through a tree as well as in stone. When we are gone we may be remembered for a little while, but a tree will lift its face to the sun for hundreds of years and people yet unborn will find peace as they walk on sacred ground beneath its branches. What a lovely thought that your 'memory tree' will be enjoyed by generations of people yet to come and that you are leaving behind such a rich legacy on the earth – because the leaves of your tree will cleanse the air and its roots sustain the soil. Amongst its branches the birds will build their nests and the bees will find nourishing nectar. In this environmentally challenging time what a splendid gift to leave on the planet when we depart.

Too Late

Lough Derg is somewhere you go to be starved, stupefied from lack of sleep, frozen by the cold, or, if the weather is warm, eaten alive by midges. Why would one go there? Why do we swim across oceans, climb mountains or run marathons? There are no answers to some questions. However, on my first visit to Lough Derg – motivated by curiosity and during which I questioned my sanity – I picked up a leaflet the words of which I have never forgotten. It made such an impression on me that the words imprinted themselves on my mind and I still remember them even now when the little leaflet itself is long gone.

> We have careful words for the stranger
> And smiles for the sometimes guest
> But for our own the bitter tone
> Though we love our own the best…

…How many go forth in the morning

Who never come home at night

And hearts have broken

For harsh words spoken

That sorrow can never put right.

On first reading, this may come across as a mere morning squabble. But as you reread you realise that it could well apply to bigger family differences and could be about much more than a trivial morning irritation. My grandmother had a very down-to-earth analysis of these situations when she pronounced: 'When two dogs have a fight, the best-bred dog walks away.'

Some family feuds can go on for years, and the longer they last the more difficult they are to resolve. Then someone dies and the opportunity to build bridges is gone forever. I sometimes visualise someone looking with regret into the grave of a family member with whom they have had a row and to whom they have not spoken for years – too late then to repair the damage by reaching out the hand of forgiveness.

Experts tell us that most family feuds happen around the times of weddings and funerals. Emotions

are running high and old sores come to the surface. Sometimes the split can be about money, land or wills. But often it can be about something very trivial. One man told me that their family row began with a rotten banana – a young wife complained that her sister-in-law had brought her bad bananas when she was in hospital. And it snowballed from there. Another family fell out over an old shed, and even when the shed was long gone the row smouldered on.

All these situations resulted in siblings ignoring each other and, even more chilling, children falling out with their parents – though a family split is often not about just one thing but a combination of many little things. There was great wisdom in the old biblical advice: 'Let not the sun go down upon your anger.'

Hold Fast to Dreams

Embossed on a little bronze plaque in my kitchen is the quote: 'Imagination is evidence of the divine.' And one of the offshoots of our imagination must surely be dreams. They seem to self-seed in the depths of our brains and imaginations, and it is only when they are in full flight that we realise they have taken off – and with that comes the irrepressible urge to rise with them. It is really important for our inner well-being to hold onto them and not let them die because they are the rich source that stimulates a plan of action.

Such was the case with the dream of commemorating the Charter School Children. You may never have heard of the Charter Schools and, indeed, neither would I but for the fact that in Innishannon we once

had one. When I came to live here in 1961 the cross-roads at the western end of the village were known as Charter School Cross; that old placename kept the story of the Charter School Children alive in the village and it is a pity that it is no longer in use because with it went a bit of our local history. But the story of the Charter School Children stayed imprinted on the back pages of my mind.

So what exactly were the Charter Schools and who were the Charter School Children? This is a strand of almost forgotten Irish history. In 1730 King George II issued a Royal Charter to set up the Charter Schools of Ireland to educate poor Protestant children and to convert Catholic children to Protestantism – the Royal Court perceived 'popery' as undermining law and order in Ireland. But because poverty was then rampant in Ireland, children of all denominations ended up in these schools, which provided bed and board as well as teaching. These residential schools, run by the local Protestant Church, took in girls and boys, from babies to the age of fourteen. They aimed to train these children for the trades – largely farmwork and housework. But the Charter Schools were often very badly run and the children neglected. They were the forerunners of the industrial schools and orphanages that followed later. The Charter Schools survived until 1830 when the National School system, that we still have today, was set up. Nowadays the memory of those Charter School children has totally faded from the pages of our history.

But sometimes life has a strange way of looking back at itself and picking up lost historical threads, and voices long-gone can make themselves heard across the ages. In 1984 we set up *Innishannon Candlelight*, a journal to record our local oral history. We had no ambitions other than that. However, as the years went on and we got our financial act together, we began to sprout other dreams. We used the funds engendered by the magazine to create longterm projects to record our historic past. From this came the sculpture of the horse and rider at the eastern entrance to the village, depicting the origins of Innishannon as the first river crossing into West Cork on the upper reaches of Kinsale harbour. Also the sculpture of the Blacksmith to celebrate the old forge that had graced the western end of the village for generations.

Then the voices of the Charter School Children began to call across the centuries to us. These forgotten children cried out to be remembered. It is surely one of the indefinable mysteries of life that we have in us the need to honour our past, no matter how sad or tragic. The Famine commemorations and the many monuments to our tragic Civil War are evidence to this. And so, not surprisingly, the dream to commemorate the Charter School Children was ignited and the journey to put wings under that dream has begun.

And hopefully on some future date when you drive through Innishannon into West Cork you will be saluted by a sculpture of the Charter School Children on the site where they once lived. And you will know then that a dream has been realised.

I See His Blood upon the Rose

Words from the soul of a writer may radiate their way into the inner being of a reader and once absorbed may forever colour the lens through which that reader views the world. One of the first poems I learnt in school had a profound effect on how I viewed the world. This was Joseph Mary Plunkett's 'I See His Blood upon the Rose'.

The poet was describing my own surroundings growing up on a remote farm in an unpolluted natural world and surrounded by people with a deeply religious sense of their world. This poem caused my young mind to marry the divine and the natural in a very easy, uncomplicated way. Going to school across many fields I was often the first to open a farm gate or climb over a ditch and stand in awe at the appearance

of a large field which yesterday had been green but was now blanketed under a tablecloth of crystal-white snow. And then Plunkett's words flowed into my mind enabling me to better absorb and appreciate what had taken place overnight. A mysterious hand had been at work and I felt that I was standing on holy ground.

In pre-electric rural Ireland the stars and moon were our companions of the night and their brilliant splendour bathed the dark, mysterious countryside in pools of light. Divine rays were pouring down on us. Even our surrounding trees were part of the divine journey as Plunkett encompassed them into the crucifixion and the crowning with thorns. On visits to nearby Ballybunion where thundering waves ploughed beneath towering cliffs, for me the poem blended divine and natural forces into a mysterious dance. He encompassed all in wonder and beauty, and this comes to mind in moments of quiet contemplation.

I see his blood upon the rose
And in the stars the glory of his eyes,
His body gleams amid eternal snows,
His tears fall from the skies.

I see his face in every flower;
The thunder and the singing of the birds
Are but his voice – and carven by his power
Rocks are his written words.

All pathways by his feet are worn
His strong heart stirs the ever-beating sea,
His crown of thorns is twined with every thorn,
His cross is every tree.

Later, when I became a gardener, Plunkett's words laced that world too with mystery. You never walked alone along early-morning, cobweb-linked garden paths without feeling that you were not alone. And along the way, dew-laden roses caused you to wonder at the miracles you were encountering. Joseph Mary Plunkett enriched my life, as indeed he did that of many others – and he continues to do so.

Going to the Well

Before piped water flowed into old farmhouses, water was drawn in buckets from wells in fields beside the houses. One might think that there was nothing to be learned from the drawing of water out of an old well, but the reaction of the well to the drawing off of water is a never-forgotten experience because a well is, in some way, representative of our own inner pool of creativity.

The inner recesses of our well at home were deep, enclosed and secretive, and everything around it was green. Even the large pale grey stone at the entrance was fringed along the outside with frills of green moss, and the dark water inside reflected the mossy arched stones overhead. But the arching moss turned a rich brown in the dark inner reflections of the water. When you knelt on the flat warm stone outside and peered into the well, your image wavered down and was swallowed into its cool brown interiors.

Once you plunged the white enamel bucket into these dark depths, the water at first resisted but then gave a audible gulp of surrender and overflowed into the empty bucket. And as the bucket eased upwards you sensed the well immediately refilling from the unplumbed depth of its deep reserves.

She lifts the bucket
Of clear spring water
From the deep brown well.
Before she rests it
On the flat stone outside,
The well has refilled,
Gurgling up from the
Bowels of the earth,
Refreshed by use
Like her own pool
Of creativity.

The well needed that act of drawing off water to stimulate its depths. Without this, the well would have gone stagnant. Like that well water, the inner creative

pool, if never stimulated, may forever remain stagnant. Creativity generates creativity.

We sometimes limit our interpretation of creativity to the artistic pursuits of art, music and writing, but creativity also flows forth in the more mundanely perceived pursuits of baking, knitting, stitching, woodwork, gardening and many, many more activities. And when we are engaged in any of these engrossing creative pursuits all is well with our inner and, indeed, our outer world.

Fresh Flowers

It is Lá Fhéile Bríde and I am trying to recall the intricacies of making a St Brigid's cross – and remembering going down to the river on the home farm beside which a rushy glen provided everything for the making of a Brigid's cross. In one of our old schoolbooks at that time was an image of a cloaked figure of St Brigid and underneath that picture was the title 'Mary of the Gael'. But unfortunately, since then we have somehow relegated Mary of the Gael to the backbenches while St Patrick has moved forward into the limelight.

This year, however, St Brigid has flexed her saintly muscles and stepped out of the shadows and has been given her own special day. RTE made an entire programme about her and as a result of that programme a 'St Brigid's Blessing' from The Book of Kildare found its way to me.

Brigid's Blessing

May Brigid

bless the house

wherein you dwell,

bless every fireside

every wall, every door,

bless every heart

that beats beneath its roof,

bless every hand

that toils to bring it joy

bless every foot

that walks its portals through.

May Brigid

bless the house

that shelters you.

But also to celebrate St Brigid's Day I have a large jug of daffodils glowing on my kitchen table, brought to me this morning by my good friend, Mary. They light up the kitchen and my inner being. Is there anything more life-enhancing than a bunch of fresh flowers, especially daffodils? But behind these daffodils is a story.

Every St Brigid's day our mutual friend Maureen arrived with a bunch of daffodils, sometimes accompanied by a St Brigid's cross, and if I was not at home when she called I came back to find them glowing on the table. But early last year she went to the heavenly garden, and this year Mary remembered to celebrate St Brigid and Maureen in the daffodils.

The following verse of mine was Maureen's favourite and one day she presented me with a framed copy done in calligraphy, which is now on my kitchen dresser beside 'Brigid's Blessing'.

Give me a bunch
Of dew-fresh flowers,
What if they will not last?
I cannot live in the future
The present is all I ask.

It is loving reminder of a friend who lived in the moment and gifted many of us with an awareness of the treasury of wonderful moments.

Few joys compare to that of meandering through a garden with a friend gathering up flowers that catch your fancy. When a colourful, scented armful is collected into a glorious bunch they never fail to light up a day. Isn't the expression 'The earth laughs in flowers' heart-lifting? Because so do we. Every summer here in Innishannon we host a 'Gardens and Galleries' day when artists and gardeners throw open their doors and gates to the public – and what a glorious occasion it is. Wandering around from garden to garden fills the visitors with delight and by evening there isn't a scowl to be seen, only smiling faces all around. People exchange gardening tips and slips, and sometimes come away full of gardening enthusiasm and fresh ideas. Gardening guru Charlie Wilkins tells us that you visit other people's gardens to steal – to steal good gardening ideas.

If you are lucky enough to be given a bunch of flowers by a gardening friend from their own garden you are truly blessed. They are gifting us with their time, love and labour. A trinity of blessings! Every time the eye falls on those flowers they stimulate a smile and light up your day.

Today, Mary's daffodils bring joy to my heart and there is more joy to come as after school six-year-old

Tim arrives with a St Brigid's cross that he has made in school. It is so good to see the younger generation continuing this age-old tradition. Mary of the Gael is certainly spreading her blessings around on her feast day.

Kindness

Kindness is one of the great blessings that oils the wheels of life. When we are in the bad place as a result of bereavement, illness or a family upheaval, the kindness of another can help us lick ourselves back to wholeness. Somebody who will take the time to sit and listen and not feel the need to share their own story. A good listener whom you trust is a priceless treasure.

The warmth of your kindness
Kept me in my mind;
Its worth could not be measured,
It had goodness undefined;
You held out a caring hand
When I was full of pain;
You thawed my frozen being
And made me live again.

I love the story of the son who rang his father with the announcement, 'Dad, I'm in big trouble', and the father's first question was, 'Criminal or terminal?' When the son answered, 'Neither', the father pronounced, 'Sortable.'

But no matter what trauma confronts us, be they sortable or unsortable, we need the kindness of others. It is one of life's healing poultices.

Kindness is a language which the deaf can hear and the blind can see.

Needs

I was sitting under a tree on the side of a hilly field down on the home farm. My children were young, my workplace action-packed, and my mother had got a stroke and was being cared for at home by my brother and his wife. Three of us within driving distance were helping out with the caring. This is a dilemma in which the middle generation can often find themselves, sandwiched between the needs of their children and their parents, and often, too, a demanding job. You discover then that anyone who tells you that the home-caring of parents is no bother, never did it. There comes a time when it can all be too much and exhaustion sets in. And your needs cry out to be met. This was my condition. I wrote about it to help calm my spirit.

Give me space

To roll out my mind

So that I can open

Locked corners

Where lost thoughts

Are hidden.

I need time

In a quiet place

To walk around

The outer edges

Of my being,

To pick up

Fragmented pieces,

To put my self

Back together again.

On that clear sunny morning while my mother slept after a restless night, I crept through the fields and sat under a tree. There I found the space and time to unpack my brain and ease the knots out of my mind.

The quietness of the fields spread out around me like a calming blanket. Gradually I emptied my brain and laid out all the tightly packed clutter on the grass around me until eventually my head was empty and its encompassing bands eased. Then very, very slowly peace and quiet gradually seeped into my being. Mother Earth was mothering me.

A Wet Day Woman

Y ou know, taking time out to reflect or contem-
plate does not always bring calmness or call up
pleasant thoughts or memories. Sometimes you find yourself dwelling on something or someone you find really
irritating or annoying. I express my irritation with moaners
in these lines I call 'Wet Day Woman'.

My sister Reese came up with this title as she railed
about a woman who drove her to distraction because she
was forever complaining. Reese believed that 'You could if
you thought you could', whereas this person believed that
you certainly could not!

> All her days were wet ones
> And all her thoughts were sad;
> And any time you met her
> You would regret you had.
> She'd depress you drip by drip

And leave you feeling low;
Oh she is a wet day woman
And will be always so.

Have you ever met someone who on their departure left you feeling less well? They exude gloom like a grey fog and leave you with some of its tendrils encompassing you. They enjoy misery. And the person who coined the idiom 'misery loves misery' must have done so after an encounter with one of these. If you have unavoidable regular meetings with one you may endeavour, on spotting them, to run, or, if that is impossible, to steel yourself to withstand the cloak of pessimism in which you know they will endeavour to enshroud you. And despite your best efforts you invariably feel on their departure that a little light has gone out of your world.

When we were young and moaned too long about something my father would say in exasperation, 'Ah don't be doing Bridgeen Connie Mac on it!' We all knew who he meant because our neighbour, Bridgeen, loved going to wakes and funerals where she would have a great time being miserable with the mourners. She would have been in her element if she had lived in the days when they had

professional wailers at the wakes.

My sister Reese christened her complainer the 'wet day woman' and her term became a joke in our family. One of my friends who is definitely not in the wet day category, queried on reading this poem, 'Is that me you had in mind?' But I think if you are in the wet day category you never perceive yourself as such.

Do you know any wet day women? Or men? Because this malaise is certainly not confined to the female of the species. There is one male politician who, as soon as he comes on TV, pours forth such a waterfall of misery that I immediately switch him off. So maybe one day I will write to my wet day politician and send him a copy of this poem, changing the title to: 'A Wet Day Man'.

A Cornerstone

Some people will never be heard of outside their own place but within that place they are the threads that darn a community together. Ellie was one such person. Her mother and grandmother had been the chapel women here, and Ellie and her sister Nonie carried on the tradition. When Nonie, as the result of a stroke, was confined to a wheelchair, Ellie, despite the fact that by then she was in her mid-eighties, took care of her while still stoically carrying on with all her other commitments.

They lived in a little house just below the church with a small sweetshop attached, where the school-children trooped in and out on their way up and down to school. The children enjoyed long chats with Ellie, who had wonderful communication skills despite being very deaf. The children loved her. Ellie also opened up the dispensary for the doctor every day and kept it

clean and tidy. Every morning she trudged up the hill to the church wearing her long brown coat with her pudding-bowl brown hat pulled down firmly over her ears. She opened the church for 8.30 Mass and once the altar was ready she plonked her brown, solid figure on the front seat. She was as regular as clockwork and as much part of our place as the church steeple. When she died suddenly she left a gaping gap.

'Good and faithful servant'
Said the wreath upon her grave.
It was an apt description
For all the hours she gave,
To the care of our church
And the daily parish round;
Before any bell would toll
There Ellie would be found.

For decades she had decorated the church for the first holy communions and confirmations, and even in her later years she still trained the altar boys with exactness and precision. Priests with different personalities came and went, but with Ellie they all toed the line. Neither was she impressed by bishops in their embroidered finery. Bishops could cause a bit of flurry at confirmation time, with priests getting a little flustered, but Ellie was not in the least bit impressed by their eminence and high headgear.

But she loved all the fuss for the weddings, especially if it was a local family that she liked – but, oh boy, if they took away the flowers after the ceremony she was not impressed and had no hesitation in saying so: they should be left in the church for everyone to enjoy.

She ran funerals like clockwork and as a hearse came up the hill to the church she waited in the front porch and knew exactly how long it would take for the coffin to make it in through the back door.

The church was her palace
Where she laboured every day,
But the graveyard was her kingdom
And there she had her say.
She knew what every headstone read
And where Kate and Mary lay
And if they were fly-by-nights
Or had substance in their day.

Filed away in her head was the location of every family grave and she was a walking encyclopaedia of parish burial records. One time a family without prior consultation with Ellie inadvertently buried a person in the wrong grave, and this only came to light when the hosting family pointed out the error. Ellie solved that problem with the minimum of fuss. She simply arranged for both families to come late one night and transfer the coffin to its proper resting place. Today this transaction would probably necessitate a court order and an expensive unwinding of a lengthy legal tangle. Ellie's 'due process' eliminated all this and probably saved the family a lot of money. But she got very upset with families who did not look after their parents' grave because she loved it when people cared.

But then one winter's morning the church door was still locked when people arrived for Mass. During the night Ellie had suddenly been taken ill and was whisked away to hospital. Shock waves went around the village. With Ellie gone, Nonie would have to be taken into care. The children too were upset to find the door of their little sweet haven locked and their old friend gone.

Ellie died that day and with her went the tradition of the chapel woman in Innishannon. She and Nonie and their mother and grandmother before them had cared for the church as if it was an extension of their own home. They washed and ironed the church linen and kept track of all records.

Like so many Irish families, many of Ellie and Nonie's siblings had emigrated to America in their youth and years later a teenage college student who lived next door to one of their brothers was touring Europe and came to visit Ellie and Nonie. This resulted in an amazing friendship flowering between these unrelated women of totally different generations.

Simultaneously, a love affair with Innishannon blossomed in the heart of the young American, which resulted in this wonderful lady, now in her seventies, making regular visits with her family back to Innishannon where she picks up the strands of friendships formed over the years. Also, the descendants of Ellie's long-gone siblings continue to return and visit their family grave and renew the connections with the people of Innishannon, who still remember their great-aunts. So Ellie, though long gone, continues to enrich her own place. I have fond memories of her as I walk around the church grounds she cared for so well. How could I not?

Sport

Yesterday I watched Rachael Blackmore ride the gallant *Honeysuckle* to victory, sweeping forward in a wave of overwhelming racing goodwill. The win would help ease the bereavement pain of the de Bromhead family whose young son had died so tragically in a riding accident a year before. As Rachael and *Honeysuckle* shot past the winning line you could feel a crescendo of goodwill and support for the grieving family sweep over a packed Cheltenham. Old rivalries and competitiveness were put aside in a great wash of human sympathy. As I watched, tears ran down my face. It was sport at its very best. A rare moment when the human spirit superseded competitiveness.

The following day, commentators Ruby Walsh and A.P. McCoy mused on this phenomenon and also on the amazing spectacle of the magnificent rainbow that had appeared at the de Bromhead funeral and then

came again in Cheltenham when Rachael and *Honey-suckle* coursed to glory. Some things are simply above and beyond human understanding.

All sports have rare golden moments of perfection when the drive to win is overtaken by a superior element in the human spirit, and if you are lucky enough to be there, or even if you are simply watching it on TV, it is a special privilege. These rare moments can also take place when sheer skill overcomes the striving for supremacy. In recent years the fierce level of competitiveness on all sporting fronts has reduced these amazing moments but when they do shine forth they are unforgettable. Gaelic games, rugby and soccer can all provide such rare experiences, but for me hurling, when played with top-class inspirational skill, can best provide such breathtaking moments.

Across our GAA parks
We watch spellbound
These fleeting deer
Play out battles

Of ferocious combat.
Blending together
The art of aerial flight
And ground warfare.

At certain moments hurling can peak into poetic ballet and it would be regrettable if the ruthless pursuit of winning should ever erode such extraordinary natural skilful achievements.

Wilding

When my life was a mad mayhem of small children, non-stop work and screaming bank managers, the garden saved my sanity. Back then in the early morning before the world woke up, I would slip quietly out of bed and creep noiselessly down the stairs, careful not to disturb the rare stillness of that early-morning peace shortly to be shattered by a search for lost socks, unmade lunches and general chaos. Before all this enveloping tide of overwhelming demands crashed in around me there was need for a coping pool of peace to be formed. The path to this pool of peace led out into the garden and the following thoughts:

> Let me steal five minutes
> To welcome in the dawn,
> To touch its dewy fingers

As they creep across the lawn,

To watch beneath a misty tree

The sun roll back the night

Its beams transforming darkness

Into soft translucent light.

To hear the birds awaken

With delight to meet their day

Let their happiness infuse me

To greet my day their way.

Let this tranquil scene give balance

To the busy day ahead

To create a tranquil pool

For withdrawal inside my head.

This garden that Uncle Jacky had planted and nurtured, and where his calm spirit still prevails, had been entrusted to my inexperienced hands and over the years has taught me many things. Our relationship was one of give and take. I took care of it and it took care of me.

These days, however, I need the garden more than the garden needs me. So we are slowing down and mellowing together into an easier pace of life. Our garden music has changed from a quickstep to a slow waltz. I no longer spend hours on my knees striving for perfection, and my garden and I have decided that a wilding waltz is the way to go. A blind eye is often turned to weeds, and flowers who, like myself, are gone past their flowering peak are left to fade gracefully away at their own pace. I have become a tolerant gardener, taking more time to appreciate and enjoy my surroundings.

I lie on the grass
Beneath a tree,
The sky peeps down
Through the leaves at me;

It's cool in here
On this warm day
A pale green haven
In the sun's hot ray.

Close to the Earth

Ag Críost on síol, ag Críost on Fómhair
In iothlainn Dé go dtugtar sinn.
Ag Críost an Mhuir, Ag Críost on t-iasc;
I líonta Dé got gscastar sinn.
Ó fhás to h-aois, is ó aois go bás,
Do dhá láimh, a Chríost, anall tharainn.
Ó bhás go críoch, ní críoch ach athfhás,
I bPárthas na ngrás go rabhaimid.

[Christ's is the seed, Christ's is the crop,
in the barn of God may we be brought.
Christ's is the sea, Christ's is the fish,
in the nets of God may we be caught.
From growth to age, from age to death,
Thy two arms, O Christ, about us.
From death to end, not end but rebirth,
in blessed Paradise may we be.]

Churchgoers of my Catholic faith are very familiar with this piece which is sung very often at Mass. The music for the complete Mass was written in the 1960s by Seán Ó Riada, and this piece, in particular, found a home deep in people's minds. When I hear it sung it takes me right back to the land.

When you grow up on a farm the soul of the land becomes ingrained into the fibre of your being and will forever be part of who you are, much as sea people have sea salt filtered through their blood. The stillness of the fields will have knit itself into your inner fabric and always within will be a hankering to return, even for a little while, to absorb the peace of that quiet place. Having been breast-fed by the land, you are forever grateful for its nourishment, and the pull to return stays with you – to lie still on the earth and blend down into the essence of its being and your being.

Come to a quiet place,
A place so quiet
That you can hear
The grass grow.
Lie on the soft grass,

Run your fingers
Through the softness
Of its petals
And listen.

On our way home from school we climbed a steep, hilly field which we zigzagged up to ease the climb and yet, having reached the top, we lay down in a long row and rolled back down again just for the sheer fun of rolling and bumping down along the grassy tufts of wildflowers along the way. Then we zigzagged back up again. Breathless after the second climb we lay out along the hilltop in recovery like a flock of exhausted geese, in preparation for rolling back down again.

My days of rolling down hilly fields are long gone, but there are still little corners of quiet to which I can retreat to absorb the surrounding peace. In our old graveyard here in Innishannon, which dates back to the twelfth century and has an idyllic riverside location overlooked by woods, we have recently placed a seat. Sitting on this seat in the shelter of the ancient tower surrounded by past generations of all denominations, including French Huguenots, is to be absorbed by peace and timelessness. Leaning against the old tower, like a soft dark green caterpillar, is an ancient yew and on the other side a large beech spreads out its leaved branches like a pirouetting ballerina. Old head-stones mellowed by age rest between the hillocks of this ancient place. It is a perfect spot to simply sit and think restful thoughts while listening to the birds who are putting on a concert for their one-woman audience. Seats in places like this are an invitation to come and sit awhile.

How nice to sit and think awhile
Of little things to make you smile…

Tread Softly

In my remembering moments I sometimes think about the power of history, as we are surrounded by it and it never goes away. The long tendrils of past events live on, often for a very long time. This is especially so when anniversaries arise. During year 2022–23 we celebrate the centenary of our civil war. But maybe 'celebrate' is not the right choice of word – maybe 'remember' or possibly 'not remember' would be better. Celebrating the centenary of the 1916 Rising was never going to be a problem as back then we all stood shoulder to shoulder in a common cause, so 1916 was always going to be a unified remembrance, a remembrance carried out with dignity and restraint. All agreed in retrospect that the 1916 commemoration was handled with great decorum and appropriateness.

Commemorating our civil war, however, was going to be a whole different ballgame and was never going to be easy. Even the fact that we avoided calling it a 'civil war' in the first place, opting instead for 'The Troubles' reveals our difficulty with the whole reality. I wonder was the term 'The Troubles' in some way connected to the expression of 'Sorry for your troubles', which was the old Irish funeral verbal balm for grieving people. By 1922 patriotism had turned to fanaticism and families split into different camps. It was a terrible time, with atrocities on both sides. Maybe it helped that by the time the centenary came around the two opposing parties of the civil war were finally in shared government together. A national healing had taken place.

Also, some very sensitively written books had come on the market prior to the occasion helping us to better understand that complicated time. *Wounds* by Fergal Keane dealt with his own intricate family entanglement, and the title of Diarmaid Ferriter's book, *Between Two Hells*, speaks for itself. Nearer to home for us in Innishannon was Liz Gillis's book, *The Hales Brothers*, about locals who took different sides in the war.

How were local remembrances going to be held throughout the country without ruffling patriotic feathers? And even more important were the sensitivities of local families whose great-grandparents, or even grandparents, had been embroiled in the conflict. These ancestors had dreams and there is never a good time to trample on dreams, as WB Yeats reminds us:

Had I the heavens' embroidered cloths,
Enwrought with golden and silver light,
The blue and the dim and the dark cloths
Of night and light and the half light,
I would spread the cloths under your feet:
But I, being poor, have only my dreams;
I have spread my dreams under your feet;
Tread softly because you tread on my dreams.

Buried here at the back of our ancient historic graveyard lies one such dreamer who later became a victim. Sean Hales was shot dead outside the newly formed Dáil in December 1922 and was brought home to be buried in his family plot here in Innishannon. Our old graveyard, where Sean Hales lies behind its ruined church, has had a chequered history, passing down through the centuries from one religious denomination to another, but through all that turmoil it still remained the resting place for all creeds. It is tucked away in a hidden corner on the banks of the river Bandon overlooked by Dromkeen Wood at the eastern end of our village, a hallowed resting place for all, and now filled with peace and birdsong.

Over the years our local Tidy Towns group have struggled against the natural weathering elements of erosion which battered these old ruins, but eventually, with the help of local muscle and government grant-aids, the ruined church and graveyard were restored and by 2022 were almost in a fit state to host a commemoration.

Before the commemoration, however, the customary 'Let's call a meeting' procedure evolved, in which you accumulate the usual talkers, doers and pontificators. Because we are the local grafters, a representative from Tidy Towns was invited on board, and we were glad to be involved. Following 'Let's call a meeting' in Innishannon, the next step is usually 'Let's call a *meitheal*', and that is when the real work begins. During 2022 we had three *meitheal* days in the old graveyard, culminating with the final one in late November, and on each of those days the sun shone for the work and the sociable sharing of tea and goodies that were part of the effort.

Members of the Hales family, one of whom brought the expertise of his landscape gardening, came from all over to help. A grandson of Sean Hales, bearing the same name and who now with his wife and family farms the home place, drew loads of topsoil to create flowerbeds in the adjacent parking area and the local gravel pit donated gravel and all that was necessary to make the whole area look good. On the laneway down to the old graveyard was an old farm cart planted with flowers which in recent years had begun to show signs of fragility, so its carer, Willie, replaced it with a new handmade model which gave a fresh, vibrant look to the entrance. It was a case of all hands on deck for this commemoration.

For the Hales family and the local community it was a coming together to pay a fitting tribute to a man who had paid the ultimate price and was part of our troubled past. The commemoration day dawned freezing cold and frosty so we gathered in clusters on the slopes around the Hales family plot wrapped up in the warmest of winter woollies. It was a beautiful, simple, prayerful wreath-laying ceremony, which the different generations of the Hales family laced with music and song, and during which showers of leaves from the overhanging trees drifted softly down, blanketing the grave in a golden glow.

And I shall hear, though soft you tread above me,
And all my grave will warmer, sweeter be…

Men with Scythes

Our current graveyard is a sunny, south-facing, hilly, humpy-bumpy assortment of headstones stretching around the church, which on a fine day makes for an interesting walkabout. It is a pleasure to ramble around there as it is beautifully maintained by a group of volunteers who come every week to clean, trim and edge. The leader of this group is Paddy, who treats this graveyard as he would his own garden, and most evenings he and other volunteers are busy along the paths and between the stones. The fact that the area is not flat and orderly adds interest to the layout though it makes maintenance much more challenging. However, that does not appear to deter the helpers and the additional bonus of having the overall place looking good is that it causes other people to be attentive to their own little patch.

The accompanying necessary but boring tarmac-adam carpark is made easier on the eye by the giant beech trees, adding interest to its bland black face, and the surrounding housing estates are eclipsed by trees and hedges. Aren't trees invaluable for creating pleasant vistas for the eye? Here in Innishannon we may not be Capability Brown, but we have been truly blessed by the generosity of nature.

And after school every day this hilly corner is filled with the shouts and laughter of the children from the nearby school as they play around the stones awaiting collection by parents. An ideal place at the end of life to rest weary bones.

> When I die
> Don't bury me
> In a military style
> Well-kept cemetery
> Where everyone
> Lies in rows
> Of well organised
> Parallel toes…

But many years ago before our present voluntary group came together to keep the graveyard in order we had instead a big once-a-year clean-up. Then it was a case of rounding up the men with scythes who would come early in summer. These elderly men worked steadily in a certain scything rhythm which caused the grass, on contact with the blade, to give a yielding sigh and then fall back easily in folds behind the scythe. These men were unhurried and took regular breaks when they leant against the stones and sometimes discussed the resident of the grave below, who might have been an old friend.

When the graveyard became overgrown
And headstones were buried in grass
Then they came,
The men with scythes,
Weather-beaten farming men
Who worked steadily
At their own pace.
Edged and cut
With the calm determination
Of those who endlessly
Work the fields…

Now all those men with scythes are resting beneath the stones they once cleared of briars and the next generation continues the work in their way.

Stored Summer

We don't have to be outdoors in a beautiful place to be touched by spurts of joy. It can happen in our own kitchens. In today's world of processed foods, a jar of pure Irish honey shines forth with the clarity of pure goodness. Legally you cannot put a 'pure Irish honey' label on your honey pot without such being the case. This statement guarantees one hundred percent that it is what it says on the jar, thus ensuring that the bees' goodness isn't tampered with or diluted by another substance before it reaches you. The bees have worked diligently for many months to produce this jar of honey and deserve to have their hard work safeguarded and the result appreciated in its pure entirety.

Having such a treasure stored in your kitchen cupboard brings summer sunshine into grey winter days. My first reaction on easing the lid off a jar of honey is to deeply inhale its goodness. This sniff of stored summer takes me out into aromatic fields:

> Bridal hedges of whitethorn
> Cascade on to green fields.
> Under bulging wings
> The gliding bees
> Collect their nectar,
> Bearing it back
> To humming hives.

Clover, whitethorn or wildflower honey all embody their own sources and once you ease off the cover and smell that golden goodness you are wafted out into summer meadows. Having grown up in a bee-keeping household, my respect and appreciation for the goodness of pure honey has never faded, and now reaching into my kitchen cupboard on a cold grey winter's morning and bringing forth a pot of gleaming golden local honey causes the sun to shine on the bleakest of days.

Earth Woman

Hamlet declared 'Frailty, thy name is woman', but many of the country women of my childhood stood in strong contrast to that statement. Those women of the land, which was a hard taskmaster, were not bowed by it but succeeded in drawing nurture and strength from its depths. They worked hard, both in the house and out in the yard caring for the fowl and animals – and often, too, out in the fields where they set and picked potatoes, saved the hay and bound the corn. They went to the bog and helped bring home turf for the open fire, over which they cooked for large families, and beside which at night they sewed and knitted to keep their families warm. They lived closed to the earth.

Earth Woman
She was as real
As the dark brown
Bank of tiered turf
With the promise
Of warmer days.

Reeks of turf were stacked behind each house and in these reeks the sods of turf were layered to support each other, helping to shelter the house from the cold and snow of winter. Also, turf provided much-needed winter warmth inside the house. Maybe in some inscrutable way their reeks of turf reflected these women.

She was as solid
As a great oak,
Unbending with
The winds that blow.
She was as strong
As the hard rocks
That weather the
Crushing waves.

Often these women were formed by the hard landscape from which they wrested a living and many in the process had to develop tough coping skills, but inside were as warm and caring as the mothering animals they looked after.

Farm women drew sustenance from the earth, which in turn drained and empowered them. They were as deep and inscrutable as the land they farmed and the animals they reared. Strong bonds were often forged with other women, often nurtured during childbirth when they supported each other and sat with each other through labour pains. Our rural roots stretch back to the land and these strong women were our maternal ancestors.

Some single women braved farm life alone and had to hold their ground sometimes against the odds. But these women had the genes of warring ancestors in their veins and were not easily cowed. Hopefully this poem encapsulates them.

> Two buckets balanced you
> As you drew feed to farm animals;
> Hands a map of ravines and ridges

Reflected your farm.

You bought land and held boundaries

Against grabbing neighbours.

Each night you knelt to say your prayers

To a God who demanded as much of you

As you did of yourself.

Back to Simplicity

My religious beliefs and rituals mean a lot to me and I sometimes think about the changes that have happened in the Church in my lifetime. Our Church has gone from being a powerful storm to a gentle breeze. But where in the first place did that powerful storm come from? Could it be that anything that is suppressed for a long time will eventually erupt into a ferocious storm?

That is what happened in Ireland with the domination by an outside power and the suppression of rights and beliefs by penal laws when priests were targeted as outlaws and Mass had to be celebrated in isolated places. With the removal of that imperial dominance, a fever of suppressed religious fervour flooded the land and while it achieved much it also caused untold damage, in time replacing the original implacable suppresser with another implacable suppresser.

Years ago I was quite angry with the Church and puzzled by its attitudes. I wrote this:

Clergyman all dressed in black
What a mighty church is at your back.
We are taught that by your hand
We must be led to our promised land.
Jesus is locked in your institutions
Of ancient laws and resolutions,
Buried so deep and out of sight
Sometimes we cannot see the light
Behind huge walls that cost so much
Where simple things are out of touch.

During that period of religious exuberance and dominance much was achieved by great people in the building and running of many hospitals and schools, but in the process tainted megalomaniacs emerged, spoiling these great achievements. And because the voice of the ordinary people was silenced, the new liberator eventually turned into the suppressor. The unimaginable, or maybe the inevitable, happened because with power come dominance and corruption. And in this process we almost lost what we had set out to achieve.

But through all these troubled times the silent people soldiered on, circumventing their now-controlling Church as best they could and continuing to follow their instinctive needs to connect with a power greater than themselves and their Church. Many connected with God in the silence of quiet places.

Is Jesus gone from off the altar
Catching fish down by the water?
Is He with the birds and trees,
Gathering honey with the bees?
Could it be in this simple way
That God meant man to kneel and pray?

Today's renewed and contrite Church is on its knees, which is not a bad place for a Church to be. Its saving grace is its remaining dedicated faithful priests who, despite being elderly and depleted in numbers, are often doing trojan work and are much appreciated and loved by the people. The previous dead wood has been pruned away and the dated old autocratic skin is being slowly eroded. Hopefully a bright new spirit is

evolving. In time, women may take their long-awaited place, and married priests be incorporated back into the fold. Is it a case of the mills of God grind slowly but grind exceedingly well?

Uplift

To be fully present, body and mind, so as to totally absorb the depths of any experience is a rare and wonderful thing. So often I am physically there, but my mind is somewhere else. Then it is a case of 'casting pearls before swine' because not having completely absorbed what has actually happened right there in front of me, I come away with nothing. When you are fully present you come away wonderfully enriched by an experience. One morning recently this happened for me in our quiet church at early-morning Mass. Somehow the words spoken had a special resonance and came through to me in a very full way.

Today I heard
And saw
For the first time:

The earth
The human
The divine.

The mystery of what I had experienced that morning stayed with me and enriched the remainder of my day. I did not fully understand what it was I had experienced but that was all right because experiences beyond our understanding can sometimes be the wings that float us into the unfathomable meanings of life. And on such occasions a poem can best capture those fleeting moments. A lot of us have problems with poetry probably due to the fact that we had it drilled into us in school, but a poem can condense in a few lines what it may take a page of prose to encapsulate, or indeed a lot of conversation and explanations to clarify. A poem can capture an experience and allow it to be revisited on subsequent readings – a little bit like putting a thought into a deep freeze to be thawed out again later. But it does not always have to be on solemn occasions that this happens. When Seamus Heaney wrote about peeling potatoes with his mother he captured one of those rare and precious never-to-be-forgotten childhood moments. Children are blessed with the innate ability to be wholly present in the Now. But sometimes we adults need words to help us. I find this little prayer said at times after morning Mass in our church does just that:

> May the Lord support us all day long
> Till the shadows lengthen
> And the evening comes
> And the busy world is hushed
> And the fever of life is over
> And our work is done…

Sometimes the profundity of Church liturgy and sacred music can takes us into an inner depth of our own being, seldom visited. As we sit in silence on solemn occasions we are sometimes gifted with rare insights into unfathomable inner terrain. These rare and intimate experiences can only be absorbed in silence.

After the Funeral

Sooner or later grief comes knocking on everyone's door and drags us along the grief road. And until we have walked in those shoes we have no idea of the immensity of its devastation. Then all our preconceived notions about grief are blown apart and previous beliefs prove meaningless. Very slowly you lick yourself back into wholeness, occasionally eased by unexpected stepping stones that may appear along the way, sometimes helped by others who have walked in the grief shoes, and especially by the sheer kindness and goodness of understanding friends.

Grief does not end
With the funeral
But goes on and on
Down a dark road.
Help me to find my way

Along this scary tunnel
Through this place of pain
That is my new world.

Over the days of the funeral you go into auto-pilot because that is the only way you can cope. The funeral rituals crack into action and in a strange way are a help because your world has crumbled into confusion, and rituals bring a certain order into the chaos. You say and do things of which afterwards you may have no recall, but for some unfathomable reason other trivial details cling to your mind.

Unbelievably, despite shaking hands with large numbers of people at a funeral whom you may not even remember, you can actually miss certain people that you would have liked to have been there but were not. Crazy! I experienced this when my brother-in-law died suddenly at a young age of a heart attack, throwing us all into absolute turmoil, and the night after the funeral my sister, in the midst of all her devastation, wondered why a particular person had not come. His presence would have brought comfort in her desolation. So, 'rational' does not apply in grief.

And when they are all gone home
And the shoulder of desolation
Nudges in my dark window,
And the cold arms of reality
Tighten their grip around me,
Will you remember then
To pick up the phone
And take time to listen,
As grief like a waterfall
Pours over me
And I struggle to survive
In my pit of black despair?

Sometimes in grief you do a lot of your crying at night. At such times I have found that when I closed my bedroom door I felt my tears were mine alone and could flow freely as they would not upset anyone else. But if the night is unendurably long, the thought of a friend at the end of a phone is a great comfort. Even if you never actually ring them.

And in the cold grey dawn
When I am going demented
With darkness and demons
Can I call you then?
And will you listen
And assure me
That I am not crazy?

Understanding friends in the weeks after a death are a great comfort. Right then the last person you need is a 'Wet Day Woman'! A good listener is invaluable because it is in going back over everything that you slowly begin to realise what has actually happened. It helps the grim reality to slowly soak in.

Will you come and visit
And sit awhile with me
So that we can talk
And the warmth of
Your kindly presence
May bring a little ease
And I might learn to live
In my scary new world?

When Steve MacDonogh, who, for over twenty years was my friend and publisher, asked me to write a book on grief I refused at first. Steve had seen me struggle through grief and felt that I could write about it. He pointed out that many of our books on grieving were written by people from other cultures and that we Irish better understand our own grief road. Eventually I agreed and worked my way through the writing. Maybe true for Tolstoy who said something like: 'Writing is best when we leave a little bit of our own flesh in the ink pot.'

Steve edited the manuscript of *And Time Stood Still* but then, just before publication, he died suddenly. And when the book, which dealt with grieving, was eventually published by O'Brien Press who took over Brandon, the last chapter of that book was the story of Steve. And during those bleak years of many deaths I discovered the wisdom of Shakespeare's words: 'The friends thou hast and their adoption tried, grapple them to thy soul with hoops of steel.'

A cold November day
She came in the door
Exuding warmth and comfort.
'The sun will shine again,'
She told me gently.

As we sat by a warm fire
On that frozen day
She melted for a little while
My inner ice.

She was a constant caller
Who walked with me along
The road of grief.
She had been there
And knew the way,
A friend who had learned
How to be a friend.

Morning Walk

Sometimes in the morning I like to don walking boots and head out of the village and across the bridge to Dromkeen Wood because

> A calm wood
> Clears the head
> Of crushed clutter.

As I walk over the bridge towards the wood I lean over the railing and watch the water churning below. The current of this tidal river on the upper reaches of Kinsale Harbour is forever changing. You may find yourself watching for the flash of fins in the swirling water. Sometimes a still fisherman stands wader-deep in water expertly casting his line. The silent stillness of a fisherman waiting patiently is a calming sight. The waters of this river, edged on either side by wooded hills, is a reflection of trees and sky.

Despite the non-stop traffic thundering along behind me on this main road into West Cork, the view from here is a picture of peace. When there is a lull in the traffic I make it to the other side of the bridge and look up-stream. Here the water is more serene, and the ducks and swans avail of this stillness. The swans float along majestically while the ducks are head-down and tails-up in constant activity.

Before heading into the wood I meander down a little pathway inside the bridge leading on to the riverbank. Down here one can view the old stone bridge beneath the new iron model piggybacking on top of it. The old stone arches of this bridge breathe the age and elegance of another era. Through the smooth stone arches reflected in the water you can view the curving, wooded river banks beyond.

Then into the wood I go to be immersed in the stillness breathed by its great trees.

Tall quiet trees
On curving slopes
Unlock the mind.

Along winding paths
Of lichened stumps
And mossy mounds
Circling choruses
Of chirping birds
Retune your thinking.

The trees in here are not in military formation because in between the upright trees and the fallen ones, others tilt sideways seeking support from their neighbours, and along the way crumbling branches and fallen, moss-wrapped elders lean across each other, sprouting lichen, ferns and new life. Here the fallen, aged and ageless provide a haven for bird, animal and human life.

I emerge with
A mind sprouting
Fresh new shoots.
And a deep gratitude
To creation
And all those
Who plant trees.

A Soft Day

Today is the first day of May. On this day, in earlier times, Christian and pagan beliefs blended to invoke blessings for good or evil. We were told that going out at dawn to wash our faces in the morning dew and run through high meadow grass brought you good luck for the year. But, though little talked about, we also gleaned that bad luck, known as '*piseogs*', could be inflicted on a troublesome neighbour by casting evil wishes and unsavoury items on their land. In our home we erected May altars, with statues adorned with apple blossoms from our old apple tree and bluebells from the nearby wooded fairy fort – but leaving outside the whitethorn, which though draped in white veils over surrounding ditches and looking beautiful, was deemed to bring bad luck into the house. On Mayday ancient beliefs and traditional customs came alive and old Ireland peeped in the door.

It was the day too when the young calves were released from the confines of their winter stalls and ran, high-tailed, down the field, exulting in the open spaces – and we children ran after them, also exulting in this new-found freedom.

I love May! This is the month that firmly bangs the door on the cold face of winter. April can be a bit pernickety and not quite sure if she is coming or going, but May has her act together and is up and facing straight into summer. This was the month when we as children finally got the long-begged-for permission to peel off our long, black knitted stockings and throw aside our heavy leather boots and run barefoot to school. Oh the glorious freedom of feeling the wet grass beneath our feet and the warm dew running down our bare legs and between our toes. Winifred M Letts captures that delight:

A Soft Day

A soft day, thank God!

A wind from the south

With a honeyed mouth;

A scent of drenching leaves,

Briar and beech and lime,

White elder-flower and thyme

And the soaking grass smells sweet,

Crushed by my two bare feet,

While the rain drips

Drips, drips, drips from the eaves.

A soft day, thank God!

The hills wear a shroud

Of silver cloud;

The web the spider weaves

Is a glittering net;

The woodland path is wet,

And the soaking earth smells sweet

Under my two bare feet,

And the rain drips,

Drips, drips, drips from the leaves.

Isn't it just magical when you step into such a shared experience! Then you are walking with another.

But back to the present! Having rolled out of bed this morning I headed up the hill to Mass and the car park was half-full of cars when normally there are only about a half-dozen. Must be an anniversary, I thought, and sure enough there in the church was Jimmy, whose wonderful wife Margaret, a regular church goer, had succumbed to cancer last May. I smile to see the rows of children and grandchildren and think: Margaret you surely left a great surge of belief and loyalty behind you. Probably, like all our children and grandchildren, they might not be regular church attendees, but they were here today for Margaret and Jimmy. It was heart-warming to see that level of comforting family support.

After Mass we all traipsed out and chatted, remembering Margaret. There is more to religion than what goes on inside the church doors. Then we scattered around and visited family graves. I met Jimmy along one path. 'Alice,' he asked, 'are we having Gardens and Galleries this year?' 'Hopefully,' I told him, glad that despite his grieving he was interested enough to ask.

'Probably around mid-July.' 'Oh good, that will give me time enough to get my record selection lined up.'

As I walked home I felt glad that we were again holding our annual Gardens and Galleries day, an annual village fund-raiser, in which Jimmy, who is superb musician and also into gramophone recitals, plays a selection from his own wonderful collection in the local Rohu's Country Market, where we all love listening to it. This is what community is all about – being there to support each other in unseen ways when the going is tough.

Back home I decide that it is breakfast-in-the-garden weather. The tulip heads are beginning to fan themselves out in a final bow, like departing ballerinas at the end of a performance, though some of the latecomers are still standing upright to attention. And the bluebells are gloriously holding centre-stage in a riotous swirl of blue. When they are like this they look very, very good, and it is best then not to think of the ever-increasing residue of cast-offs they leave behind on departure. This is not the time to allow that thought to dampen my present delight in them. Today is about enjoying their blue exuberance. Yesterday I visited them in Dromkeen Wood where, because it is hilly terrain, they have the scope to spread themselves out in free abandonment, climbing up the hills and flowing down the slopes in blue waves. They wash the entire wood in a haze of blue. Magnificent!

Likewise, here in my garden they defy any efforts to curb their gallop into every corner. They would take over completely if I let them. But best now to just sit in their midst and enjoy them.

Later I carry the breakfast tray into the back porch and as I reach up to the shelf above the window for my garden diary, I also find, and take down, another little book. In 1995 my sister Ellen and I were visiting Niagara on the Lake, a town in Canada, and while meandering around a bookshop Ellen picked up this little book and handed it to me, saying: 'I'm getting this for you.' The title was *Meditations for Women Who Do Too Much*.

What I like about it is that it takes each day and offers a thought for that day. They can be grand thoughts or very simple little ones. I take it back out into the garden now and look for today's date. Today, Mayday, the text is about taking an ordinary day and

celebrating that. Sometimes we take an ordinary day for granted until it's snatched away from us by some sudden and unexpected trauma. Then we may look back longingly at that ordinary day and regret our lack of appreciation for its ordinariness. So maybe now was the time to celebrate this normal day with nothing spectacular happening. Maybe no day is ordinary, really. Maybe they are all special if we appreciate them.

So I decide to appreciate this ordinary day with nothing extraordinary happening.

Jim

Just across the road
Jim lived in a shed;
It wasn't very big,
Just enough to hold his bed.

J im was part of the village. He worked around the parish with different farmers and came back at night to his shed in the corner of a small yard between houses along the street. He was part of a group of men who usually gathered around the village corner every night and he spent his nights in the local pub with them. During the day, when he was no longer working on farms, he sat on a windowsill along the street and chatted to passers-by. A kindly neighbour fed him, so he had enough to eat and he was never lonely.

I always felt that Jim and his companions were the original Community Watch as they kept track of all village activities and knew who had passed by and who had taken the bus to Cork or Bandon. If you wanted to know anything about local activities you only had to ask Jim and his friends.

But we all worried about him sleeping in the cold of his shed. We felt something should be done for him. Jim was getting old. Then came a very cold winter and we all felt bad about Jim and convinced ourselves, and Jim, that he would be better off in kinder conditions. So he went into a home. He seemed to be better off. But well-meaning people who think we know best can sometimes make big mistakes, as I was about to discover.

But when I went to see him
Jim's face a story told
His body was dry and warm
But his eyes were lost and cold.

Jim died in September,
Died in a spotless bed
But Jim had died six months before,
The day he left the shed.

He died in a warm, clean bed, but I knew that he had really died when he left his shed and his village. Maybe in some ways we are like deep-rooted old trees that cannot in later years be dug up and replanted. Jim and an ancient oak had a lot in common:

> My roots grow deep
> Into the warm earth.
> But pull up my roots
> And my whole being will break.

The Meaning of
Life

This issue has puzzled the wisest of minds since life began. But is it a case of 'the answer, my friend, is blowing in the wind'? Maybe nobody knows.

When Gay Byrne decided to tackle this 'big question' on RTE with a programme of the same name, I found it intriguing to listen to his searching questions and the many answers they engendered. I watched every programme, fascinated by the variety of people who took part and all the different points of view. Believers and non-believers discussed their different ideas, some ruffling viewers' feathers with their opinion that God was a monster and staunch believers probably irritating people who thought otherwise. It made for very interesting viewing. Then when Gay went on to where maybe the answer is to be found, the torch of enquiry was passed on to Joe Duffy.

I had the greatest respect and admiration for the people who took part in that programme because appearing on it was akin to taking your clothes off in public, but in this case it was your mental clothes you were shedding, and this could be far more intimidating. How would it be to do that, I wondered? And then, all of a sudden, I was about to find out!

An email arrived from O'Brien Press to say that RTE had been in touch asking if I would be willing to do the programme. If I was willing, I could travel to Dublin and record it on an afternoon when Joe Duffy would be there, or if I wanted to stay put they would come south some Saturday.

At this stage of my life I am a bit like Mohammed, preferring the mountain to come to me, so home ground would be my choice. But the big question was how did I feel about doing the programme at all? Having watched so many others do it, I was well aware that it would be pretty challenging, but I was also hugely curious as to how I would handle it. The meaning of life has always intrigued me. But I had no answers, so why would I go on the programme? But then neither did anyone else have answers, it seemed. And if I did not do it would I forever be curious as to how I would have handled it? My husband Gabriel had always said that it was what he had failed to do in life he most regretted rather than what he had done. So, curiosity got the better of me and I decided to go for it.

I got back to O'Brien Press to say Yes, I would do the programme and that my choice of venue was Innishannon. Then a request came from RTE researcher Gareth Williams for a chat to put the bones of the programme together. Researchers are seldom seen but they are the vital network linking the presenters and the viewers. Gareth Williams was of a different generation to me and born in the inner city, but we spoke the same language and our hour-and-a-half chat on the phone flew by and was filled with interesting exchanges and a lot of fun. Gareth was a top-class communicator. It augured well for the programme but he would not be coming to Innishannon on 15 April, so I would be in the hands of Aisling, the producer, whom I hadn't yet met.

As the days went by I tried to put the thought of

doing the programme out of my head and kept myself busy in the garden and decluttering the house, which is a constant work-in-progress here because the more immersed you are in voluntary organisations the more clutter you acquire. Unfortunately I overdid the work in the garden and one cold day overstretched myself shifting pots, and ended up crippled with aches and pains and a nasty cold. That put manners on me and made me realise that if I did not want to do the programme from a prone position a certain amount of pacing needed to be introduced. So I went on a 'Slow me down, Lord', practice.

During the week before the programme my mind turned to clothes and my hair for the day of the recording. I decided to simply wash my hair that morning when showering, but that simple solution was overruled by my daughter: 'Mom, it's television! Will you for God's sake get you hair done properly that morning!' That is the plus of daughters – they keep you up to speed with life.

The next problem was what to wear, so I went through my wardrobe with a critical eye but found little joy in there. Covid had not been conducive to retail therapy, so most items were a bit jaded-looking, and anything I considered as a possibility, my daughter dismissed as 'out of the question'. Every item in her wardrobe was either too short, too long or too revealing. At my time of life, graceful, delicate robing eases the gaze of the beholder! Luckily I have a niece who is a good dresser, so she was my next port of call and after a long perusal through her wardrobe I came home with a possibility. With a few days to go, we were down to the wire, so one morning I donned Eileen's outfit and decided this was it, and she later called and confirmed that it fitted the bill.

Then Aisling rang to say that she would be down on the Friday before the Saturday filming to check the layout of the house – in other words to case the joint! There would be a few camera operators, a sound engineer and a make-up artist, and, of course, Aisling herself, and Joe to do the interview. They would be staying overnight in the Innishannon Hotel. I did a blitz on the house to reduce clutter and by Friday afternoon had all my ducks in a row, having also made an 'Aunty Peg apple cake' and ordered his super sandwiches for the crew from Tom in Rohu's Country Market at the end of the village. On Friday afternoon Aisling arrived with the crew. They checked out the front room, shifted some of the furniture into the *seomra ciúin* out of their way, and pronounced themselves ready to roll at nine o'clock the following morning.

Did I sleep well the night before? Not bad, actually! And looking back now, I think that it was a case of 'fools rush in where angels fear to tread'. I had no idea of the recording marathon involved in making a half-hour programme. Joe was absolutely superb, but this was a programme that cut close to the bone and as we recorded I revisited the deaths of beloved family members because this programme was all about the meaning of life and that, of course, inevitably deals with death too. By the time the two-hour recording was completed I felt as if I had run a marathon. How had it gone? I had no idea! To me it was a patchwork picture of bits and pieces of my life. I didn't know what would emerge when the two hours' recording was edited down to a half-hour.

Then we all gathered around the kitchen table and enjoyed Tom's sandwiches and the apple cake. The programme would not be going on air for months, so I decided it was best just to forget about it for now.

When my children were small and watching a scary programme on TV they hid behind the couch and peeped over the top when they thought it was safe. I imagine that is how I will be watching 'The Meaning of Life' when it eventually comes on TV in the autumn.

Other books by Alice Taylor:

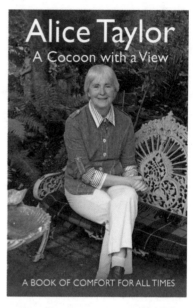

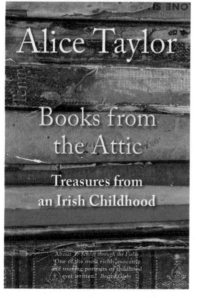

Alice Taylor

From the bestselling author of
To School through the Fields

And Life Lights Up
MOMENTS THAT MATTER

Alice Taylor

From the bestselling author of
To School through the Fields

Home for
Christmas

Alice Taylor

And Time Stood Still
From the bestselling author of
To School Through The Fields

Alice Taylor

The Women
From the bestselling author of
To School Through The Fields

Alice Taylor

Do You Remember?

Alice Taylor

About *Do You Remember?*
'Magical ... Reading the book,
I felt a faint ache in my heart ...
Essential reading.'
Irish Independent

As Time Goes By

Alice Taylor

About *To School through the Fields*
'One of the most richly evocative
and moving portraits of
childhood ever
written.'
Boston Globe

Tea for One
A Celebration of Little Things

Alice Taylor

'It's like being wrapped up in a
patchwork quilt of Nana's love ...
Absolutely gorgeous'
*C103's Cork Today
with Patricia Messinger*

The Nana

*See the O'Brien Press website,
obrien.ie, for a full list*